# Anatosaurus

**Written by David White**
**Illustrated by Pam Mara**

**Library of Congress Cataloging-in-Publication Data**

White, David, 1952 July 13–
  Anatosaurus.

  Summary: Describes the physical characteristics, habits, and natural
environment of the plant-eating Anatosaurus.
  1. Anatosaurus—Juvenile literature.
[1. Anatosaurus.  2. Dinosaurs]  I. Mara, Pamela, ill.  II. Title.
QE862.065W45  1988      567.9'7      87-36960
ISBN  0-86592-520-8

**Rourke Enterprises, Inc.**
Vero Beach, FL 32964

Quetzalcoatlus

Parasaurolphus

Deinosuchus

Spinosaurus

Oviraptor

# Anatosaurus

Pachycephalosaurus

Anatosaurus

Struthiomimus

Scolosaurus

Rutiodon

Psittacosaurus

As the sun filtered through the trees of the forest, Anatosaurus awoke. Nearby lay the rest of the herd. Anatosaurus sniffed the morning air, and smelled the scent of flowers at the forest edge. He was hungry and thirsty.

He stood on his hind legs, using his great tail to balance himself, and bit off the branch of an oak. Anatosaurus chewed slowly. His strong teeth could grind any foliage, even pine needles, to make a meal that he could digest. He browsed quietly among the branches of the tree. The forest was his home and his source of food. In it, he could find all the leaves and fruit he wanted.

When he was young, Anatosaurus lived near the water. His mother hatched her eggs on the shore of a lake, so that the hatchlings could run to the water whenever there was danger. Then he had lived on water weeds, sucking them up from the water.

When he grew older and his teeth became
strong, he moved away from the lake and into the
forest. There was always plenty to eat. The forest
contained every kind of tree – pines and firs, oaks, ash,
poplars, sycamores, willows, maples, and birch.

After a morning of grazing, Anatosaurus lay down and dozed in the midday heat. He did not sleep, however. There was always the danger of attack by other animals, especially the fierce meat-eaters.

Luckily, Anatosaurus had sharp eyes and good hearing. Most important of all, he had a keen sense of smell. While it was still far away, he could smell the scent of another animal in the wind. This gave him plenty of warning.

Today, though, there was no wind. The forest was hot and still. Anatosaurus could hear the grunting of the herd as it browsed contentedly in the heat. Suddenly, the grunting changed to a loud croaking. Something had frightened the herd. Animals began to run off through the trees. Anatosaurus got up on his hind legs. He could run fastest this way.

Then the cause of all the panic burst into sight. It was Deinonychus, known as "terrible claw." Deinonychus was only a small animal, but his sickle-like claw made him a fearsome opponent. With his claw, he could wound and even kill animals much larger than himself.

Anatosaurus was no match for Deinonychus, so he did the only thing he could. He ran. He ran through the dense undergrowth of shrubs and small trees toward the lake. He knew instinctively that the water would protect him.

Anatosaurus was as suited to the water as to the land. He had webbed feet and a long flat-sided tail to help him swim fast. Once he reached the lake, he knew he would be safe.

As he ran, he could hear Deinonychus behind him. He looked anxiously for a sign of the lake. With his great weight, Anatosaurus was beginning to get tired. If he stopped for breath, he knew that Deinonychus would be on his back, tearing at him with his terrible sickle-claw.

Suddenly, the lake came into view. Anatosaurus bounded across the shore and plunged into the water. He swam away from the land with a few powerful sweeps of his tail. Deinonychus could only stand at the water's edge and watch his prey escape. Then he turned away and loped off in search of other prey.

Afterwards, Anatosaurus returned to the shore. The lakeside was now calm and peaceful. Palaeotringa, long-legged wading birds, probed the sand for shellfish and worms. Plegadornis stood at the water's edge, watching for frogs and water beetles.

Graculavus, who had been diving for fish, shook his wings dry as he perched on a rock by the lake.

Anatosaurus found plenty of food around the lakeside. He ate pistia, or water lettuce, and trapa, water chestnut. If he waded into the lake, he could sample some salvinia, a floating fern.

As Anatosaurus took his pick of the succulent plants, a herd of Brachylophosaurus wandered onto the shore. They were harmless, plant-eating creatures like himself. Yet suddenly Anatosaurus heard the harsh clash of bone against bone, as Brachylophosaurus battled with Brachylophosaurus.

It was a trial of strength, rather than a fight. One of the younger members of the herd had challenged the herd leader to a contest. The two animals stood face to face. Then they pressed their face plates, made of solid bone, against each other. The winner was the one who forced the other to give way. He could then become the leader of the herd.

Anatosaurus stopped browsing among the greenery to watch the contest. At first, it looked as though the young Brachylophosaurus would win. Then the experience of the leader began to tell. The older Brachylophosaurus started to push the younger one back.

Just as it seemed that the leader would win, a terrifying roar sent the birds of the lake flying into the air. Out of the forest stalked Tyrannosaurus. He saw the herd of Brachylophosaurs and broke into a run. The great creature took short, awkward steps, giving the herd time to scatter. Anatosaurus fled with them.

Tyrannosaurus watched the herd scattering in front of him. He was looking for the weakest and the slowest animal. Finally, he made his move, darting in among the Brachylophosaurs. Anatosaurus saw his chance and ran for the edge of the forest.

He looked back. Tyrannosaurus stood over a
Brachylophosaurus, tearing at it with his vicious teeth.
The rest of the herd had escaped, and so had Anatosaurus.

In the late afternoon, Anatosaurus rejoined his own herd in the oak forest. He found them browsing peacefully. Anatosaurus was tired and hungry by now. He reached up to the branches of an oak tree and began to eat. The running had tired him. Soon he lay down, curled up his great body in the forest undergrowth, and slept. The light faded slowly in the forest.

# Anatosaurus and the Late Cretaceous World

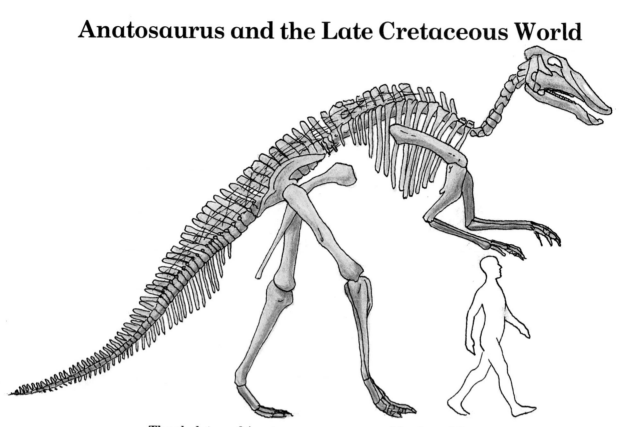

**The skeleton of Anatosaurus compared in size with a man**

### The time of Anatosaurus

The Mesozoic Era, known as the Age of the Dinosaurs, lasted from 225 million years ago to 65 million years ago. Palaeontologists divide this age in to three periods: the Triassic, the Jurassic and the Cretaceous. Anatosaurus lived in the second half of the Cretaceous period, some 70 million years ago. We know this because bones and even pieces of mummified skin have been found in the rocks that were laid down in that period. Anatosaurus lived right up to the end of the Mesozoic Era, until the point when, mysteriously, all dinosaur life on Earth ended.

### The land of Anatosaurus

Towards the end of the Age of the Dinosaurs, the world began to look more like it does today. The two supercontinents of Laurasia and Gondwanaland had broken up to form the present continents, which were separated from each other by vast oceans. Dinosaurs were no longer free to roam the world.

Anatosaurus lived in great numbers in North America. The land looked very different then. It was generally flatter. The central range of mountains had not yet been formed. It may also have been intersected by a vast inland sea which extended from the north to the south. The story in this book takes place in what is now New Jersey.

### The family tree of Anatosaurus

Anatosaurus was one of the first of the hadrosaurs, or "duck-billed" dinosaurs. Hadrosaurs were by far the most successful of all the ornithopods living in the Late Cretaceous period. The first hadrosaur, Batractosaurus, lived in Mongolia 100 million years ago. By 60 million years ago they had spread to Asia Europe and North America.

There were three main groups or branches of the hadrosaurs: the flat-headed hadrosaurs, the solid-crested hadrosaurs, and the remarkable hollow-crested hadrosaurs. (Scientists are not certain what these crests of hollow bone were for, but they think they may have acted as recognition signals). The group that changed least during the 40 million years of their existence were the flat-headed hadrosaurs, among them Anatosaurus.

## Other plant eaters

Plant-eating hadrosaurs were the most successful dinosaurs of the Cretaceous period. They completely dominated the North American and Canadian forests, browsing among the trees at the forest's edge. Brachylophosaurus, who appears in the story, was one of them. Brachylophosaurus had a strong bony face-plate which was probably used in combat with members of the herd. However, hadrosaurs, like all plant-eaters, were docile creatures, and they would not have used their hardened skulls to fight off predatory meat-eaters.

## The meat eaters

If the hadrosaurs had been allowed to browse undisturbed, they would have stripped the forests bare. They were prevented from doing so by the meat-eating dinosaurs, the lizard-hipped carnosaurs, who attained a terrifying power and size during the Cretaceous period. The best known is Tyrannosaurus Rex, who appears in the story. This was the largest flesh eater of all time, almost 15 metres long and weighing ten tons. However Deinonychus, a far smaller carnosaur, was probably more fearsome even than Tyrannosaurus.

Although it was only two metres long, it wielded a sickle-shaped claw which enabled it to overcome plant-eaters much larger than itself.

## Birds and plants

Much of the bird and plant life of the Cretaceous period would have been recognizable to us today. Besides the older trees, such as conifers and ginkgoes, there were pines, firs, oaks, ash, poplars, maples and sycamores. Among the birds, Graculavus looked much like a present day cormorant and Plegadornis resembled a heron or a stork.

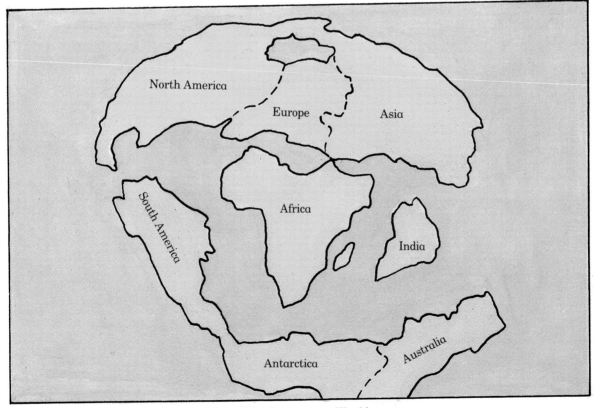

**Map of the Cretaceous World**